HOLINESS

HOLINESS

GOD'S PLAN FOR FULLNESS OF LIFE

HENRY BLACKABY

THOMAS NELSON PUBLISHERS®
Nashville

A Division of Thomas Nelson, Inc.
www.ThomasNelson.com

Published in Nashville, Tennessee, by Thomas Nelson, Inc.

Unless otherwise indicated, Scripture quotations are from THE NEW KING JAMES VERSION. Copyright © 1979, 1980, 1982 by Thomas Nelson, Inc., Publishers.

Scripture quotations noted NIV are from the HOLY BIBLE: NEW INTERNATIONAL VERSION®. Copyright © 1973, 1978, 1984 by International Bible Society. Used by permission of Zondervan Publishing House. All rights reserved.

Library of Congress Cataloging-in-Publication Data

Blackaby, Henry T., 1935–
    Holiness : God's plan for fullness of life / Henry Blackaby & Kerry
Skinner.
        p. cm.
    ISBN 0-8499-2085-X
    1. Christian life. 2. Holiness—Christianity. I. Skinner, Kerry L.,
1955– II. Title.
BV4509.5.B546 2003
234'.8—dc21   2003012108

Printed in the United States of America

6 QW 06 05

To our fourteen grandchildren
as they pursue diligently God's
will in their lives.

*Mike, Daniel, Carrie, Erin, Matthew,
Conor, Christa, Stephen, Sarah, Emily,
Douglas, Anne, Elizabeth, and Joshua.*

Contents

INTRODUCTION

THESE MESSAGES ARE THE HEART OF MY PRESENT ministry. Preached in one form or another, these Truths have developed in my life over many years. They are my *life-messages* to God's people, as God calls us to renewal, revival, and spiritual awakening. These Truths first began to make a deep impression on my life as a young boy. I can remember listening to my layman father teach and preach. He began a church in a dance hall in a very sinful city on the northern coast of British Columbia, Canada. He saw broken lives in an alcohol-soaked city. He wept before the Lord over the condition of the people. Time and again he preached passionately on sin, repentance, the fear of God, and holiness. Sin in the lives of desperate people overwhelmed him as he lived out his Christian life with integrity. He remained true in his personal holiness. Our family also lived our lives under the deep conviction of the return of the Lord and its accompanying accountability. All this left a deep impression on my young life.

As a young man my life and message were also shaped toward repentance and revival through the many stories and pictures my family received from China during the great Shantung Revival. My aunt and uncle were missionaries in China during those awesome and exciting times of revival.

During the early days of my ministry God convinced me of His holiness and the need for His people to return to Him. God used the writings of Oswald Chambers and Duncan Campbell to impact me deeply. The year before I went to Faith Baptist Church in Saskatoon to become their pastor, Duncan Campbell had been in the city. He left a significant mark on the city and indicated God's promise of revival in Canada. This promise of revival and the witness of his godly life were some of the reasons I answered the call to minister there.

I had already felt the weight of sin and the deep need for

biblical repentance while pastoring in California during the 1960s. I trembled before God as I realized God's people no longer feared God nor sin, and no longer sought holiness. As a pastor I saw the consequences of sin in God's people. Passionately I preached and taught God's people to fear God, hate sin, and thoroughly repent before holy God and seek holiness as a way of life.

God honored the fervent and faithful proclamation of these Truths to His people. God's people did heed God's Word, and lives and families were dramatically changed. The communities where I pastored were changed in many ways, and the lost were saved. God graciously granted me the privilege of experiencing touches of real revival. My first encounter with deep and real revival was in Saskatoon, Saskatchewan in western Canada. After I had spent much time in prayer with the other pastors, God suddenly moved mightily, every night, for seven and one-half weeks! Churches were affected, and thousands of lives were touched. The effects of those days are still being felt thirty years later. During this time we saw many people saved, new churches started, and many people called into the ministry. Many churches experienced great renewal.

Later, at Howard Payne University in Texas, God allowed me to see and experience revival with the people there. This revival affected hundreds of other colleges and many seminary campuses. The Truths God had burned into my heart were being confirmed in changed lives. Again, in Ft. Collins, Colorado, I witnessed twenty-one straight hours of deep brokenness and repentance in a gathering of several thousand Campus Crusade workers. I encounter many of those changed lives as I travel all over the world.

My life has been shaped by God through these experiences of revival, and thus the heart messages of my ministry have been deepened. In this book I share what God put on my heart for His people. Today, I am passionately burdened to share these much-needed Truths with God's people:

- The loss of the *fear* of God

- Seeing *sin* from God's perspective

- The *highway of holiness*

May God continue to be gracious and grant that these words and Truths continue to draw God's people toward

Him and thus toward the experience of deep revival. My life-message continues to be toward true revival and spiritual awakening in this nation and across the world—for the glory of God!

One

THE LOSS OF THE
FEAR OF GOD

IT IS THE PEOPLE OF GOD WHO CAN TRULY SHAPE a nation. Many look to great leaders or powerful governments to shape a nation. But most likely, leaders and governments will not restore a nation once it is on the downward slide. While leaders and governments can influence a nation, there is no group of people who can determine the coming years of a nation like God's people.

As go the people of God, so goes the redemption of the world. God is therefore working mightily in His own. We are closer to either revival or judgment than we have ever been. There is not an alternative to these two. Either God's people return to God with all of their hearts, or God will judge our nation. We do not have to guess how that judgment will look or how thorough it will be. The Bible indicates how thoroughly God judges His people. Any nation that forgets God as a corporate people comes under the judgment of God. When God judged Israel, the Northern Kingdom, He completely wiped them out. When God judged Judah, the Southern Kingdom, He destroyed Jerusalem and the temple and put the people in bondage for seventy years. God also took the people in Jesus' day and scattered them so thoroughly that they did not get back together for more than nineteen hundred years, just as Jesus predicted.

As go the people of God, so goes the redemption of the world.

If we look at the history of God's dealings with His people it ought to cause us to tremble. But it is the loss of the fear of God that characterizes God's people in America today.

DEFINING REVIVAL

In 1987 there was a conference on prayer and spiritual awakening in North Carolina. The keynote speaker, Dr. J. Edwin Orr, spoke on April 21. His message was *Revival Is Like Judgment Day*. That was the last message he ever preached. The next day he passed away and went to meet his Lord whom he had served so faithfully. That message has stayed on my heart. The topic of that sermon is very consistent with the Scripture—*revival is like judgment day*.

But many of us are not thinking about judgment; we are thinking about revival. We seem to have redefined revival in our day as something different from the Scripture's definition of revival. We seem to have consistently changed the definition to the way we want it to be. We have changed God to our own image. We have changed worship, youth work, and family life to what we want. We have changed, for application in our own lives, nearly every commandment of God. We continue to break all of the Ten Commandments. If I were to take you through what the Scripture says about the Sabbath day, you would see that God's people have utterly desecrated it—that is, if you take the Scripture as the guideline for how to act on the Sabbath day. But as long as everyone does what is right in his own eyes and it is not different from anyone else, we assume, as long as God does not judge us, that things are okay. But they are not. There is an incredible heart cry for revival. I think it is a God-created cry. I think it is a cry to God such as, *Oh, God, revive us again so that Your people may rejoice in You!* I want you to understand the nature of what God is doing.

I assume as you consider this message that you do have a heart cry for revival. But understand that our nation, our churches, and our family lives need a deep personal encounter with God. We need to be reoriented back to God at every level of life. That heart cry in your life is real and personal, but your involvement in the ways of

Our nation, our churches, and our family lives need a deep personal encounter with God.

God does not come simply because you listen to a message. It comes from a deep personal and corporate processing.

When you hear the Word of God, it begins immediately a process in you to understand and respond to what God is saying. When you come face to face with God and He says something through His Word, you immediately begin to find that you must respond, *If this is what God says, then this is what I must do.*

BLESSING OR CURSE

Remember when the priests were cleaning the temple in Josiah's day and they found the Scriptures? The Scripture says, "Now it happened, when the king heard the words of the Book of the Law, that he tore his clothes" (2 Kings 22:11).

Do you remember when the priests took those Scriptures and began to read them in the presence of the king? You can find the entire story in 2 Kings 22 and 23. Suddenly the king realized for the first time what the standard had been all along and that God is not mocked. Whatever a people sow, they will reap. The king was no longer ignorant of what that would look like, because now the covenant was being read as to what God would do *if* the people followed and practiced what God said. Then in Deuteronomy 28 and Leviticus 23, the covenant listed all God asked them to do. The first part of the covenant was very positive.

The negative side of the covenant began with Deuteronomy 28:15. God said that if they did not follow what He told them, He would reverse all their blessings as a covenant people of God—chosen, encountered, instructed, and separated by Him. God then preserved in Deuteronomy 28:15–68 the awful things that would happen to a people of God if they refused to follow Him. Verse fifteen is the powerful beginning of those words:

> But it shall come to pass, if you do not obey the voice of the LORD your God, to observe carefully all His commandments and His statutes which I command you today, that all these curses will come upon you and overtake you.
>
> DEUTERONOMY 28:15

When Josiah heard that he trembled. The Spirit of God that was upon him to function as king caused his heart to be pierced. He immediately began to weep and tear his clothes. He put on sackcloth and ashes and called for the people to repent. Josiah took seriously that what God said,

He meant. He knew there were no favorites and no exceptions. He realized they were standing on the utter edge of destruction.

The problem was they had set the Scriptures over in a place where they were no longer being noticed. They were covered with debris. All the time the Scriptures were being ignored, the judgment was progressing. They were closer to God's judgment because they had lost their standard. They had lost any standard for behavior. So they would sit and discuss what they thought was acceptable to God. But it did not matter what they thought, it was what God had said that was important. Everyone was doing what was right in their own eyes, moving steadfastly toward the utter judgment of God. Judgment was coming as sure as God was there. Josiah wisely understood it. He immediately adjusted his life to God. The king called all the spiritual leaders together quickly to bring the people together and corporately repent (2 Kings 22:11–23:3).

God listened to Josiah's heart and sent word to him:

"Because your heart was tender, and you humbled yourself before the LORD when you heard what I spoke against this place and against its inhabitants, that they would become a desolation and a curse, and you tore your clothes and wept before Me, I also have heard you," says the LORD. "Surely, therefore, I will gather you to your fathers, and you shall be gathered to your grave in peace; and your eyes shall not see all the calamity which I will bring on this place."

2 KINGS 22:19–20

What happens when you come up against the Word of God? Do you tremble when God speaks? Isaiah 66:2 says, "But on this one will I look: on him who is poor and of a contrite spirit, and who trembles at My word." When was the last time you were confronted by God in His Word and literally shook like a leaf?

FEAR OF GOD/FEAR OF SIN

I made a phone call recently to a significant leader of an organization, who told me, "Henry, I am so grateful that you called. You have no idea the importance of this phone call." I had made a covenant with him to call him on a regular basis because his position of leadership was very influential.

When I asked him what was happening in his life, he said, "Never in my life have I ever been so utterly terrified. For God's reasons alone God began to deal with sin in my life. God has brought up things that I have not thought about for years and years. He has brought up things from my youth that I have never dealt with in my life—things that have affected my marriage and my assignment. God was relentless for three weeks bringing to mind what He sees as sin and how serious it is with Him. I came to the place a few days ago where I cried out to God and asked why God was doing this to me. God said to me, 'Because you have lost the fear of Me I am doing this.'"

> We are moving closer to an absolute confrontation with a God who makes no exceptions.

When you do not fear God, you will not fear sin. There is a direct relationship between a high view of God and a high view of sin. A low view of God brings a low view of sin. When there is no fear of God, there is no fear of sin. It is amazing to me the number of people who

9

can sin grievously against the Word of God. In the Old Testament, they would have been put to death for many things people do today. In the New Testament, God says it is far more serious than it was in the Old Testament. It amazes me how so many people somehow believe that as long as they do not feel that something is bad, that it is not bad—as long as they can feel okay about it, they can continue to do it. As long as God does not deal with them immediately, it must be okay. We are moving closer to an absolute confrontation with a God who makes no exceptions.

This man I had called said, "Henry, I want you to know that only in the last three weeks has God put on my heart an understanding of why we do not see revival. We do not see the hand of God moving on the people of God because we have lost the fear of God."

Later, I was in another state talking with a large group of people. Some people came up to talk with me after the meeting, and they told me what was happening in their church. They said that the church had taken a vote for a building program. The constitution of the church stated they must have a 75 percent vote to proceed. They had a 72 percent vote. They said the pastor had thrown a fit and began to berate them. He took 100 of the people and moved less than a mile down the street and was looking for a building to start another church.

When I heard that, I began to tremble. The Scripture shows that you cannot touch the body of Christ without God dealing with you severely (Acts 5:1–5).

I have listened to story after story of people who have been through church splits all over this nation. The people involved do not have a fear of God at all! They tend to comment that at least they started another church. They did not start a church—they started a religious club! God did not have anything to do with the split. The Spirit of God is never involved in a church split. Never! He is the author of unity. God's people can explain it away all they want so that they feel good about it. But when you have a church split, you cancel your right to preach the gospel of reconciliation. That church just demonstrated that the God who reconciles to Himself cannot reconcile this group of His own. What message does that give to the world? The tragedy is that there is no fear of God.

I discovered from my thirty years of pastoring that God does His work of judgment on the children. That next generation usually has nothing to do with the people of God. They marry into godless homes, they divorce, their grandchildren are hurting, and everything falls apart. Some say God did not judge them. You do not understand—He just did! God said the hearts of your children will be turned away from Him— they will not follow in His ways.

Marilynn and I have prayed from the moment our first child was born, *Oh, God, keep us holy, for the sake of our children. Keep us walking with You. Keep us a part of the building of the people of God so that our children will want to serve You also.*

My heart cry is for me and the people of God around me to come back to God's Word and let Him tell us what the standard really is.

RETURNING TO GOD

The term *revive* means "to return the life to." Lost people cannot be revived because they never had life in the first place. They first have to be saved—awakened to their lost condition. Revival is exclusively what God does to His people. When the life of God has gone from the people of God and we are content to live without the manifest presence of God—content week after week without any evidence of the presence and power of God—then we need to be revived. We need for the life of God to come back to us.

I want to give you a word picture of what it is like when the presence of God falls on His people. Have you ever been in the midst of anything like this, or is this what you have imagined from the Scripture that revival would be like?

"Behold, I send My messenger,
And he will prepare the way before Me.
And the Lord, whom you seek,
Will suddenly come to His temple,
Even the Messenger of the covenant,
In whom you delight.
Behold, He is coming,"
Says the LORD of hosts.

"But who can endure the day of His coming?
And who can stand when He appears?
For He is like a refiner's fire
And like launderers' soap.
He will sit as a refiner and a purifier of silver;
He will purify the sons of Levi,
And purge them as gold and silver,
That they may offer to the LORD
An offering in righteousness.

"Then the offering of Judah and Jerusalem

Will be pleasant to the LORD,

As in the days of old,

As in former years.

And I will come near you for judgment;

I will be a swift witness

Against sorcerers,

Against adulterers,

Against perjurers,

Against those who exploit wage earners and widows and orphans,

And against those who turn away an alien—

Because they do not fear Me,"

Says the LORD of hosts.

MALACHI 3:1–5

I was aware of a situation not long ago in which it was discovered that a pastor had rented motel rooms for a particular woman. Nobody had known about it! But it really was not true that no one knew. God was there when the pastor signed his name! When God deals with him, He will come as a witness against him. That should cause us to tremble! Things we have long hidden from the eyes of others were not done in secret from God. In revival, God shows up as a witness against us.

If you lose the fear of God, there is nothing to restrain you. Many do not believe God sees them and do not believe He is aware of the condition of their hearts. They think that if He sees them and does not stop them, that it is okay. But He does see you and may not stop you, and it is *not* okay. If the Word of God says it is sin, then it is sin.

> "For I am the LORD, I do not change;
> Therefore you are not consumed, O sons of Jacob.
> Yet from the days of your fathers
> You have gone away from My ordinances
> And have not kept them.
> Return to Me, and I will return to you,"
> Says the LORD of hosts.
> "But you said,
> 'In what way shall we return?'"

MALACHI 3:6–7 NKJV

When we hear a message that calls us to return to the Lord, God's people consistently say, *Well, wherein do I need to return? I am a Christian. I have been born again. I was baptized. I am a leader in the church. I am going to heaven when I die. What do you mean, "return to God"?*

If there is any area where God's people are disoriented, it is in this matter of repentance. If we were to talk in very serious terms about repentance, many would bow their heads and pray, *Oh, God, if there is any lost person here, I pray that they will hear this word and repent.* But God is shouting at His people saying, *It is not the lost who need to repent—it is God's people who need to repent!* We are the ones who have moved away from the Lord.

GOD IS SHOUTING AT HIS PEOPLE SAYING, *It is not the lost who need to repent—it is God's people who need to repent!* WE ARE THE ONES WHO HAVE MOVED AWAY FROM THE LORD.

So with a compassionate heart, a deeply concerned heart, God came and told the prophet Malachi to say to His people that the God whom they had been seeking would suddenly come to His temple (Mal. 3:1). When He comes in our day, no one will be able to speak except God. When God is through speaking, you will know how He sees what you have done.

Two

LOOKING AT SIN FROM GOD'S PERSPECTIVE

GOD IS CALLING HIS PEOPLE TO RETURN TO HIM and be a *highway of holiness* over which He can come to the lost world. But before we can become a highway of holiness, we must understand the issues of sin. In order to understand sin, we must see our sin from God's perspective. We must build our relationship with God in such a way that our lives can be a highway over which God reaches the rest of our nation in a great revival among God's people, and in a sweeping spiritual awakening in the hearts and lives of those who do not know Him.

There is an urgency that we carry within us. This urgency has at least two major directions. If I understand the Scriptures correctly, God will judge any nation that neglects His direction. It may very well be that we are under the judgment of God.

If I were to attempt to find the beginning of what I believe is a national neglect of God, I would return to the early 1960s. It seems as though God removed the hedge of protection from around America in that decade. We began to see unrestrained things take place from the '60s to this present day. There seems to have been nothing to hold back the tide of injustice in society. A deep departure from God in the churches has continued since that decade. It is as if the hedge of His protection has been broken down, and God is letting us experience the consequences of our own sin.

There is an urgency in the Scriptures when God says, "If My people who are called by

The salvation of the nation has little to do with Washington or Hollywood—it has to do with the people of God!

My name will humble themselves, and pray and seek My face, and turn from their wicked ways, then I will hear from heaven, and will forgive their sin and heal their land" (2 Chron. 7:14). That great passage indicates clearly that the redemption of America waits on the repentance of the people of God. The salvation of the nation has little to do with Washington or Hollywood—it has to do with the people of God! If God's people do not sense that the problem is with them, then America does not stand a chance of revival or survival. And so, understanding in ever-increasing measure what God says in His Word, we carry with us a deep sense of urgency that we are closer to the judgment of God on our nation today than we were last year.

REVIVAL AND PRAYER

Do you believe that when God's people pray that God hears, responds, and brings about a deep change? Are you helping your family and the people in your church to pray for the condition of their lives, families, church, and nation? Remember, God said, "For the eyes of the LORD run to and fro throughout the whole earth, to show Himself strong on behalf of those whose heart is loyal to Him" (2 Chron. 16:9). He also said, "The effective, fervent prayer of a righteous man avails much" (James 5:16). Jesus said, "And whatever you ask in My name [consistent with everything I have taught you], that I will do, that the Father may be glorified in the Son" (John 14:13). With these promises—with which God's people can change the course of a nation's history—what has become of prayer in your own life, in your marriage, in your family, in your church, or in your denomination?

If revival in America depended on your prayer life, would there be a revival? If you have to say, *Not my prayer life,* then you must change your prayer life. To have a renewed prayer life requires a simple matter of a personal choice. Your life is the product of choices you have made, and your church is the product of choices it has made. Your prayer meeting is a reflection of the choices you have made as a church. Our nation is a reflection of the choices that have been made by the people of God concerning their relationship with God.

That is one of the reasons why this kind of message has a sense of urgency about it. I believe there is a lot at stake. In fact, eternity is at stake for many in our nation. But, in your

In your church alone, there are enough of God's people—if they were serious with God— to turn the course of our nation.

church alone, there are enough of God's people—if they were serious with God—to turn the course of our nation.

There were only 120 people in the Upper Room who were wholly yielded to the person of Jesus Christ (Acts 1:15). God used them to turn the entire Roman empire completely upside down. In 1904 God used a young man from Wales named Evan Roberts. God broke him and shook him through a specific time of prayer—with others who had been praying across the land— and 100,000 people came to faith in Jesus Christ in six months. The great revival of 1904 began with prayer. Thousands of people ended up on the mission field as a result. Roberts, at twenty-six years old, was focused on prayer and revival, and that revival set in motion a great missionary movement.

What could God do through your life? Do you sense that America needs the mighty touch of God? Do you believe God could work through your life as He has done with others? Would you be willing to make the kind of choices required by God to be that kind of person? Your response to reading this message will be a reflection of the choices you have made concerning your Lord.

URGENCY OF THE HOUR

There is another reason why there is such urgency to being completely yielded to God in the here and now. I believe we may be the generation that is still living when the Lord Jesus returns. I believe that God may now be calling the last generation of those who will go with Him on a mission to the ends of the earth. Most of the leaders I have encountered in the last few years—whether a pastor of a local church, a leader of a ministry group, or a leader of a denomination—have joined in saying they believe with all their hearts that we may be the generation that is still living when the Lord Jesus comes back.

Do you suppose, since the Father knows the time, the day,

and the hour when He will say, *Enough—time shall be no more.*
My Son will come in the clouds, the judgment will begin, and eter-
nity will be ushered in, He could be causing an urgency in the
hearts of His people and His churches, knowing that the hour
is short and there is limited time for people to respond? Do you
believe we will face our Lord and give an account to Him for
the way in which we have lived? Do you suppose if our Father
knows the time of His coming that He may have already issued
the instruction to the Spirit of God to,

> make My people understand the urgency of the hour, that
> when they hear My Word, there will be a different kind of
> urgency in their hearts. Cause My people to understand that
> to invest their lives with the world that will pass away is not
> as important as investing their lives in the kingdom that will
> never pass away. (Paraphrase)

God is stirring the hearts of children, young people, college students, and those in midcareer with a call into missions
as never before. In recent days one foreign mission board
processed over 9,000 names of people who were inquiring
about the pursuit of foreign mission appointments. Did you

know that just a few years ago in the Southern Baptist Convention alone, more than 300,000 people volunteered for missions at home and abroad? And more than likely, within a few years, they could see 500,000 from their churches on missions to the ends of the earth.

In recent times many have said, *In an amazing way, over the last several years, God has stirred my heart and caused me to go on a mission trip. I never dreamed I would be on a mission trip in another part of the world, but something happened in my heart, and I went, and I have never been the same.* This calling of volunteers is happening all across the people of God. I do not believe this is accidental. I believe this is under the direction of God, and I believe it has something to do with the near return of our Lord. Because of these urgent times we must stand before God and His Word and see things from His perspective.

FROM THE HEAD TO THE HEART

It is not enough for God to speak to you from His Word, because all the head knowledge in the world will never change your life. When what you know in your head hits your heart you will not be able to rest day or night until God has become that way in your life.

I hear many people say, "Well, I believe Jesus is the Son of God. I believe He is the Savior of man." All the Truth believed in a person's head is also believed by all the demons in hell, yet they are one step ahead of us. At least when they know the Truth in their heads, they *tremble*. They know Jesus died for the sins of the world. They know He was the sinless Son of God. They know He was raised again. They know the power that raised Jesus from the dead has been given to every one of us who believes.

> All the Truth believed in a person's head is also believed by all the demons in hell, yet they are one step ahead of us.

They know He is interceding. They know He is coming back. There is not a Truth you and I believe in our heads that they do not believe and tremble. But the difference between the demons and us is that when we take it from our heads and let it hit our hearts, we cannot rest night or day until what God shows us in His Word is being lived out in our lives.

Second Corinthians 1:20 has made an incredible impact on my life this year. The passage says, "For all the promises of God in Him are Yes, and in Him Amen, to the glory of God through us." The moment you became united with Jesus Christ in the saving work of God through the death of His Son on the cross, every promise God ever made in this Book has become *yes* for you. Now, many of you know that in your heads, but let me tell you how to know if it has ever hit your hearts. The moment you know that promise is true, it ought to be an obsession with you to find every promise God has ever given and live it out, so God can be that way in your life. If it is in your head only, it will not change anything in life. But when you hear the blessed Lord Jesus say, "Most assuredly, I say to you, he who believes in Me, the works that I do he will do also; and *greater works* than these he will do, because I go to My Father" (John 14:12, emphasis added), and that Truth hits your heart, your life will never be the same again.

Can you imagine what would happen to change the course of America if we believed just that one promise with our hearts? And there are hundreds of promises given in the Word of God. Are you letting what you hear in your head go eighteen inches lower to your heart, and begin to change the way you live?

You and I have the greatest single possibility of making a difference because God has given us His promises. God says He will respond when we have responded: "Draw near to God and He will draw near to you" (James 4:8). Then why do we not draw near to God, and keep in that direction until we know God has drawn near to us and His presence has literally changed everything about us? You cannot be in the presence of God and remain the same. That would be absolutely impossible. The Scripture, "Draw near to God and He will draw near to you," is simple but profound.

Are you taking the promises of God and literally standing before Him until He is in you exactly as He promises in His Word? The tragedy is that many of God's people can know they are living their lives the same as the world around them without it disturbing them. Did you know that it deeply disturbs God for us to live our way instead of His way? For God's people to go their own way is called sin. The Scripture says, "Whatever is not from faith is sin" (Rom. 14:23). The

Scripture further explains, "Therefore, to him who knows to do good and does not do it, to him it is sin" (James 4:17). Another Scripture states, "Whoever commits sin also commits lawlessness, and sin is lawlessness" (1 John 3:4). One of the laws is that you, "Bear one another's burdens, and so fulfill the law of Christ" (Gal. 6:2). Sin is when you see your brother with a load, and you do not help him carry it—that is sin, and that is grievous to the heart of God.

You used to be just human, but now you are a child of the King of kings.

There is nothing I see in the Scripture that burdens the heart of God more deeply than sin in the hearts and lives of His people. So I want us to look at sin from God's perspective—not from our perspective. How does God look on sin? Scripture says sin is coming short of what God has required. That is sin. "Oh," you may say, "I'm just human." No you are not; you are indwelt by almighty God if you have been born again! You used to be just human, but now you are a child of the King of kings, indwelt as a temple of God, and now your life is not yours—it is now Christ living out His life in you. Is not that what Paul said? "I have been crucified with Christ; it is no longer I who live, but Christ lives in me; and the life which I now live in the flesh I live by faith in the Son of God, who loved me and gave Himself for me" (Gal. 2:20). That is not a figure of speech—that is a fact! For me to know that and to resist Him is sin. A definition of sin in 1 John 3:4 is that "sin is lawlessness [rebellion]." Rebellion is when one knows what God says and yet chooses not to obey. I have often said the two words that cannot go together are *No, Lord.* One of those words has to be removed. If He is Lord, there is no possibility of your saying *no.* You cannot call Him *Lord* without saying *yes.* What God is looking for are His children who constantly say, "Yes, Lord."

SIN FROM MAN'S PERSPECTIVE

There is no greater prerequisite to revival than for us to see our sin from God's perspective and deal with it immediately.

I believe I could safely say there is no stronger passage in the Bible to which we could turn and see sin from man's perspective than Psalm 51:

> Have mercy upon me, O God,
> According to Your lovingkindness;
> According to the multitude of Your tender mercies,
> Blot out my transgressions.
> Wash me thoroughly from my iniquity,
> And cleanse me from my sin.
> For I acknowledge my transgressions,
> And my sin is always before me.
> Against You, You only, have I sinned,
> And done this evil in Your sight—
> That You may be found just when You speak,
> And blameless when You judge.
> Behold, I was brought forth in iniquity,
> And in sin my mother conceived me.
> Behold, You desire truth in the inward parts,
> And in the hidden part You will make me to know wisdom.
> Purge me with hyssop, and I shall be clean;
> Wash me, and I shall be whiter than snow.

Make me hear joy and gladness,

That the bones You have broken may rejoice.

Hide Your face from my sins,

And blot out all my iniquities.

Create in me a clean heart, O God,

And renew a steadfast spirit within me.

Do not cast me away from Your presence,

And do not take Your Holy Spirit from me.

Restore to me the joy of Your salvation,

And uphold me by Your generous Spirit.

Then I will teach transgressors Your ways,

And sinners shall be converted to You.

Deliver me from the guilt of bloodshed, O God,

The God of my salvation,

And my tongue shall sing aloud of Your righteousness.

O Lord, open my lips,

And my mouth shall show forth Your praise.

For You do not desire sacrifice, or else I would give it;

You do not delight in burnt offering.

The sacrifices of God are a broken spirit,

A broken and a contrite heart—

These, O God, You will not despise.

Do good in Your good pleasure to Zion;
Build the walls of Jerusalem.
Then You shall be pleased with the sacrifices of righteousness,
With burnt offering and whole burnt offering;
Then they shall offer bulls on Your altar.

This psalm gives us a brief look at how David saw his sin. But there is no possibility that you will ever understand Psalm 51 unless you see how God caused David to see his sin from God's perspective, which was totally different from David's viewpoint.

God made David aware of his sin. David would never have seen his sin had God not granted him the understanding of it. God grants repentance. There have been many times when I have cried out, "Oh, God, would You grant Your people the capacity to understand and repent? If You do not move us toward repentance, we will continue in our own way. If You do not intervene in our lives, we will continue in our sin."

Psalm 51 was David's response to God's helping him understand that his sin was far more serious than David had given credit. This passage deals with his sin against

Bathsheba and against Uriah, her husband (2 Sam. 11:3–26;12:9–10). But you need to remember, when God sent Nathan to bring conviction to David's heart, it was probably a full year after David had committed his crime. The child from his sin of adultery had already been born before Nathan the prophet approached David. David had worked out in his heart how to deal with his sin against Bathsheba. He had worked out a scheme by which he could kill Bathsheba's husband in war and then after a normal period of mourning take her to himself as one of his wives. It was only after that long procedure that God finally sent Nathan to say, "David, you are the man!" (2 Sam. 12:7). God gave David more than a year to repent, but he did not repent. If God had not intercepted him, he probably would never have repented.

Yet God knew the essence of David's heart. And God seemed to say, "David has a heart for me. Sin has blinded him—sin has distorted his reasoning. Sin has done what I know sin will always do. But I know David's heart, and if I confront David with his sin and I bring conviction to David about his sin, he will repent, and he will return to Me, and he will be the person that I am looking for."

But hear the cry of David. He says, "Have mercy upon me, O God" (Ps. 51:1). This passage gives you a thorough picture of genuine repentance.

What is mercy? When David said, "Have mercy upon me, O God, according to Your lovingkindness; according to the multitude of Your tender mercies" (Ps. 51:1), he meant for God to deal with his sin. What is your definition of mercy? Well, my understanding of mercy is that God withholds from me what I justly deserve. Mercy is God's withholding what He has a right to do immediately. Would you want God to give you what you justly deserve?

What did David rightly deserve from God? Death. His sin deserved immediate death. When we turn to another passage, that is exactly what Nathan said to David, "The LORD also has put away your sin; you shall not die" (2 Sam. 12:13). It is as though Nathan said, "God has forgiven your sin, and you will not die. David, you could have died. God would have been absolutely just in dealing with you. David, you have got to see your sin from God's perspective."

The first cry of David was, "Have mercy upon me, O God!" As David continued his thoughts through the psalm, he used a number of different terms. He said, "Blot out my

Mercy is God's withholding what He has a right to do immediately. Would you want God to give you what you justly deserve?

transgressions" (Ps. 51:1). I can almost hear David say, "Lord, I violated clear guidelines. You said, 'Do not commit adultery,' and I did. It was specific in Your Word, and I violated it. Oh, Lord, would You blot out my transgressions?" If God did not deal with David's sin, it was all over for David. He had violated a clear command of God.

God is not merely a loving Father in the heavens; He is a righteous, holy God. Every time those who take His name violate anything He has said, it is a reflection on the name of God. It empties God of His holiness and His righteousness.

One of the great deterrents from going astray when I was a young man was my dear godly father, who was a deacon and a layman. He led more people to Jesus than any other person I have known, including myself. He worked in the business world, but he was one of the most godly men I have ever known. I knew how Dad had paid the price for integrity and righteousness in the business world.

One day my dad came to me and my two brothers and said, "Boys, I just want you to know that I spent a lifetime building meaning into my name, and wherever you go, you take my name with you. It has cost me my life to put integrity into my name; now you carry my name with you." When I was tempted and could have gone astray, I thought of my dear dad, and I said, *I couldn't do that to him. I carry his name, and Dad has a name as a godly Christian businessman. I couldn't do that to him.*

For me to sin without regard to the name I carry would be to bring the deepest pain to my father possible, for he sought to honor his Lord by the way he lived. He entrusted his name to me. If that is how I felt concerning my earthly father, how much more serious is it with my heavenly Father? He laid down His life in the life of His Son to say to the world that sin is serious with God. It cost Him His Son to take care of the sin of the world. For me to sin without reference to Him would be a major blow to my relationship with God. He does not take that lightly. Every time I carry His name and live in a sinful way, I cause scores of others to misunderstand the holiness of God.

A friend of mine, a pastor, was very active in helping others know how to live in Christ, but he began to have an affair with a lady in his church. Another friend and I went to him immediately and with all the urgency of our hearts told him to turn from his sin. He disregarded all our counsel. He not only continued that relationship, but he divorced his wife, left the church where he was pastoring, created great tragedy in the church and great sorrow with his children, and finally married this lady. A few years later I was leading a conference where I was speaking on denying yourself, taking up your cross, and following Christ. He attended that conference. Somehow God used those messages to bring him under great conviction. He said, "I've got to talk with you." We went aside, he began to weep, and he said, "Henry, this is the first time I've ever acknowledged this before anybody. I have deeply sinned against God. I have grievously dishonored my Lord. I have deeply sinned against my wife and my children and God's people. Would you pray for me?"

I said, "Oh, my brother, I will. But let me tell you how I'm going to pray. This is how I'm going to pray for you. I'm going to pray that in your returning to God He will forgive you, but that He will deal with you in such a way that anybody who sees it will be forever deterred from even thinking about committing this grievous sin." His face dropped. I turned to him and said, "I'm far more concerned about God's name than your name. I'm far more concerned about restoring God's name in the hearts of people than restoring your life. I care about you, but I want you to know I care far more about what you have done to God."

David understood sin from God's perspective and so the heart cry of David was with full understanding. David cries out, "Blot out my transgressions!" Then he says, "Wash me thoroughly from my iniquity, and cleanse me from my sin" (Ps. 51:2).

Psalm 51:7 states:

> Purge me with hyssop, and I shall be clean;
> Wash me, and I shall be whiter than snow.
> Make me hear joy and gladness,
> That the bones You have broken may rejoice.
> Hide Your face from my sins,
> And blot out all my iniquities.
>
> Create in me a clean heart, O God,
> And renew a steadfast spirit within me.

Do not cast me away from Your presence,

And do not take Your Holy Spirit from me.

PSALM 51:7–11

That is how to repent of all your sin! Do you see your sin from God's perspective? David did. David again seemed to extend all of the human language to cry unto God and say from his heart, *Oh, God, my sin—from Your perspective—is so grievous, I'm going to cry out to You with every ounce of my being until I know that You have dealt with me thoroughly and completely.* Notice then he said, "*Then* I will teach transgressors Your ways, and sinners shall be converted to You" (Ps. 51:13). When I get my life right with God, my life becomes a highway over which God can go to convince and convict others of their sin.

David then said, "For You do not desire sacrifice, or else I would give it; You do not delight in burnt offering. The sacrifices of God are a broken spirit, a broken and a contrite heart—these, O God, You will not despise" (Ps. 51:16–17). David's spirit was utterly shattered when he saw his sin from God's perspective.

But he did two other things. In Psalm 51:3–4 David said, "For

When I get my life right with God, my life becomes a highway over which God can go to convince and convict others of their sin.

I acknowledge my transgressions, and my sin is always before me. Against You, You only, have I sinned, and done this evil in Your sight." Where did David do his sin according to this Scripture? In God's sight. With God watching him and David knowing God was watching, he deliberately sinned. David acknowledged he knew it. He did not make any excuse; he did not give any reasoning. He simply said, "With You watching, I transgressed the clear guidance You have given me, and, oh, God, it was against You and You only that I have sinned. You may be found just when You speak, and blameless when You judge. Oh, God, anything that You do to deal with my sin is absolutely just. You are absolutely right. You have the right to do anything You want because sin is that serious with You."

Remember what God did; God did two major things. God said, "Now therefore, the sword shall never depart from your house, because you have despised Me, and have taken the wife of Uriah the Hittite to be your wife" (2 Sam. 12:10). All through the gospels, Jesus taught, "With the same *measure* you use, it will be *measured* to you" (Mark 4:24, emphasis added). That is the New Testament perspective. I express God's words this way: "David, you, by the sword of the Ammonites, took Uriah's life. Now I will not let a sword depart out of your home. David, your entire family is going to experience a sword in their lives because of your sin. And second, David, though I will not slay you, I will slay the child that is born because of you." How serious is sin from God's perspective?

When we look at our sin, we tend to cover it up. We say, *It is not all that bad. God is a loving God. He wouldn't deal with me this way.* If you look at the Scripture from God's point of view, then you will cry unto God the way David did. Psalm 51 gave us David's perspective; now I want you to look at this same sin from God's perspective.

SIN FROM GOD'S PERSPECTIVE

God's view of David's sin is described in 2 Samuel 12. In this chapter you will see and understand why David cried out to God so deeply, because now he saw his sin from

God's perspective. Remember, a whole year had probably passed by and David had not dealt with his sin.

I have a feeling David was just like you and me. David did not see the immediate consequences, so he did not respond to God. If we do not see the immediate consequences of our sin, we feel it is all right with God. If God does not come and deal with us severely when we know we have sinned, we will probably assume it must be all right because there have not been any consequences to our sin. But you do not have to wait for the consequences—you can know from the Word of God whether it is correct or not, or whether it is sin or not, and deal with it immediately. Do not let the sun go down on sin in your life. Do not presume on the mercy and the grace of God. Deal with sin immediately.

In many ways we have an advantage over David, although he had the same Holy Spirit. God has given us in this present day the Holy Spirit whose assignment is to make sure that we are constantly convicted when we sin. The gift of the Spirit of God is to help God's people know when they have sinned. He will bring to our remembrance the Scriptures, and He will bring to our remembrance God's standard. God will convince us of our sin and will plead with us to make it right with Him.

I want you to see why David came to such a heart cry. Nathan told David the story of a poor man who had nothing but one beautiful little ewe lamb. A rich man who had many sheep took the poor man's lamb. And David said, *That man deserves to die.*

"Then Nathan said to David, 'You are the man!'" (2 Sam. 12:7).

What God said next is absolutely crucial, because it is much more serious for us than it was for David. God was putting David's sin in the context of the grace of God. The more God does, the worse our sin.

What was David before God made him king? He was a shepherd. What distance did God take David from being a shepherd to making him king over all the people of God? God had never been so good to anybody on the face of the earth as He had been to David. So before He let him see the seriousness of his sin, He reminded David of the context of his sin. Here is my paraphrase of verses eight and nine:

David, I anointed you king over Israel, and I delivered you from the hand of Saul. David, you did not escape because you had greater ability to get out of the way of Saul. I personally intervened, and I kept you from Saul. I gave you your master's house and your master's wives into your keeping. And I gave you the house of Israel and Judah. And if that had been too little, I would have given you much more. David, there is nothing that I would have withheld from you. Now David, you sinned against the background of all My goodness to you. David, that makes your sin far worse than anyone else's, because I have never done this for anyone else, and having done all of this for you, David, when you sinned, you had to do it with the knowledge of all I had done for you.

Then Nathan said of David's sin, "Why have you despised the commandment of the LORD, to do evil in His sight?" (2 Sam. 12:9). God was saying, "David, for you to have committed the sin that you did so blatantly, you had to despise all My teachings."

You may say of your sin, "Oh, God, I did not despise Your teachings, I just fell in a moment of weakness." That is your perspective, but look at it from God's perspective. God says for a Christian to sin willingly he has to do it against all the Spirit of God has been doing to teach him the ways of God. God gave us the Holy Spirit to be our teacher—to guide us into all Truth—to teach us everything. We have the Scripture in scores of translations. We have no excuse for our sin. We have all the grace of God.

God placed me in a godly family. My grandmothers on both sides were godly people. God gave me a mother and father who walked with God with all of their hearts. They were pacesetters for my life, and they protected me and led me to know the Lord. My uncle who baptized me was in the great Shantung Revival as a missionary. I had all of that godly background. A number of my relatives graduated from Spurgeon's college in London. They started Baptist churches all over England. I have an enormous heritage. Do you understand that when I sin, I do so against the backdrop of the goodness of God? The effects would be enormous. You need to pray that God will keep my heart true to Him. He has allowed me to hold many public positions—if I were to sin, can you imagine the tragedy that would happen to those who know my life? Pray for me, that I will remain true to the Lord.

I have been trembling before the Lord as I read this, because God saw David's sin against the backdrop of God's grace. But you and I have much more than David had, because we know what happened at the cross of Jesus Christ. We know that the Son of God, though He was rich, became poor that we, through His poverty, could be made rich (2 Cor. 8:9). We know "God so loved the world [and us] that He gave His only begotten Son" (John 3:16). We know more than David did. We know it took God the life of His Son to provide us with freedom from sin. And then we know that God raised Him up and Jesus is interceding at the right hand of the Father for us. Do you know there is not one of us who sins in our lifetime who does not do it against the intercession of the Lord Jesus who is constantly at the right hand of the Father interceding for us? We sin against a lot more of the grace of God than David ever knew. Is it serious with God?

We sin against a lot more of the grace of God than David ever knew. Is it serious with God?

You need to see something else from this passage in 2 Samuel 12:10. He said, "Now therefore, the sword shall never depart from your house, because you have despised Me." God said that for a child of His to deliberately sin, he has to despise God to do it. Now, your heart and mine may reason, *That is not how I look on it.* It does not matter how you look on it; it matters how God looks on it! Revival will never come to the people of God until we see the awfulness of our sin as God sees it. It is not a light matter with God.

For David to have sinned, he had to despise the commandments of God—the teachings of the Lord. And we add to all David's knowledge all that we know in the Gospels and all that we know in the entire New Testament. We have to despise the whole New Testament to continue in our sin. God said, "You have despised Me, David" (2 Sam. 12:10). But there is even a more tender moment that has gripped my heart as I see it from God's perspective.

Read on with me to verse 12 and following: "For you did it secretly, but I will do this thing before all Israel, before the sun." It is much more serious for a leader to sin than for an average person, because they influence so many. When a leader sins, many times God does not hide it, but He announces it from the housetops. "So David said to Nathan, 'I have sinned against the LORD.' And Nathan said to David, 'The LORD also has put away your sin; you shall not die. However, because by this deed you have given great occasion to the enemies of the LORD to blaspheme, the child also who is born to you shall surely die. [David, your sin gave an occasion for all of My enemies to blaspheme My name]" (2 Sam. 12:13–14).

When I read that, I wept and wept, "Oh, God, I love You with all of my heart."

But God would say, "Then deal with sin, because there are enemies of Mine who are just waiting to find some of My children who are going to sin. And when they see you sin, or a church sin, it is going to give them great occasion to blaspheme My name."

I replied, "Oh, Lord, I did not know it was that serious."

"I know you did not," He answered, "or you wouldn't keep on sinning the way you do."

If you do not make it right with your brother, you sin against God and cause the enemies of God to blaspheme His name.

Do not give occasion for the enemies of God to blaspheme Him by the way you behave. You have the guidelines to love your brother—to prefer him over you. Read Philippians 2:5: "Let this mind be in you which was also in Christ Jesus." Let

Do not give
occasion for the
enemies of God to
blaspheme Him by
the way you behave.

your brother serve in a more prominent position. Let your brother be the chairman of the committee. You be a master servant. Do not give any occasion for the enemies of God to blaspheme the name of our Lord.

"Oh, God, do not let my life give occasion to Your enemies to blaspheme Your name." I have been weeping my heart out before God saying, "Oh, God, do not let an idle word come out of my lips. Do not let me have an unguarded moment where something comes out of my lips bringing great offense, causing the enemies of God to say, 'Oh, we have got something now. What is his God like that will not help him to live a godly life?'" And I pray, "Oh, God, help me to always remember my sin as You see it; not as I see it, but as You see it."

Some of you may be thinking, *But Henry, that is Old Testament thinking only.*

There is a New Testament passage that tells you that a New Testament Christian's sin is far more grievous to God than David's was. Hebrews 10, beginning with verse 26, gives the weight of the heart of God. Sin is failing to do what the Spirit of God tells us we must do; failing to walk by faith when He is trying to get us to trust Him and demonstrate His greatness to His children, rebelling against the commands of God by simply not even trying to know what they are, or justifying ourselves to God.

"For if we sin willfully after we have received the knowledge of the truth, there no longer remains a sacrifice for sins, but a certain fearful expectation of judgment, and fiery indignation which will devour the adversaries" (Hebrews 10:26–27). He was not talking about lost people; He was talking about God's people. Jesus essentially said, "If you're not going with Me, you're going against Me." If you deliberately are not finding where God is at work and joining Him, you are deliberately moving against Him.

"Anyone who has rejected Moses' law dies without mercy on the testimony of two or three witnesses. Of how much worse punishment, do you suppose, will he be thought worthy who has trampled the Son of God underfoot, counted the blood of the covenant by which he was sanctified a common thing, and insulted the Spirit of grace?" (Heb. 10:28–29). Those were God's people. Of how much worse punishment, do you suppose, will they be thought worthy? Then the writer of Hebrews describes how God sees the sins of the New Testament Christian. It says to me that there are three ways God says He sees my sin. He says, "Henry, for you to sin, you have to tread the Son of God under your feet. You have got to walk all over the Son of God to do it. Second, you're going to be treating as common the blood of the covenant that set you apart and sanctified you as a child of God. And third, you're going to have to insult the Spirit of Grace."

That is an awesome statement of how God sees our sin. Of how much worse punishment, do you suppose, will they be thought worthy who have trampled the Son of God underfoot, counted the blood of the covenant by which he was sanctified a common thing, and insulted the Spirit of Grace? "For we know Him who said, 'Vengeance is Mine, I will repay,' says the Lord. And again, "The LORD will judge His people" (Heb. 10:30). It is far more serious for a Christian to sin than an unbeliever, because for us to sin, we have to do it against the knowledge of the Truth. For us to continue in our sin means that we have to tread underfoot the Son of God, and we have to treat as common the blood of the covenant that set us apart as belonging to God. We also have to insult the Spirit of Grace, who has been telling us that it is sin and that we need to be careful.

He concludes by saying, "It is a fearful thing to fall into the hands of the living God" (Heb. 10:31). God is talking about us. Do you see your sin from God's perspective? Revival waits on the people of God to say,

Oh, God, forgive me. Oh, God, what have I done to You—what have I done to Your Son? How could I have continued to practice sin knowing it was sin, knowing it was not what You asked, knowing that I was not walking by faith and causing others not to walk by faith—how could I possibly have done this in the presence of all that You have shown me? I would have had to reject all of Your grace to do that. How could I have told my church, 'God will not provide,' and discouraged the hearts of God's people to take a step of faith—how could I have done that in the presence of all that You said about Your grace? And I caused others to stumble.

It is inevitable that people will experience offenses, but probably the most severe statement Jesus made, in my opinion, is, "Whoever causes one of these little ones who believe in Me to sin, it would be better for him if a millstone were hung around his neck, and he were drowned in the depth of the sea. Woe to the world because of offenses! For offenses must come, but woe to that man by whom the offense comes!" (Matt. 18:6–7).

Do you know that if you speak up in a church business meeting and some young believers are there, and you leave the impression that God is not able to help that church do His will, and you offend and turn aside some of the believers from trusting God, "It is better," God said, "for you to have a big millstone hung on your neck and dropped into the deepest part of the sea." And He continued, "If your hand or foot causes you to sin, cut it off and cast it from you. It is better for you to enter into life lame or maimed, rather than having two hands or two feet, to be cast into the everlasting fire. And if your eye causes you to sin, pluck it out and cast it from you. It is better for you to enter into life with one eye, rather than having two eyes, to be cast into hell fire" (Matt. 18:8–9). I am not saying you will lose your eternal salvation. I am just quoting what Jesus said.

How serious is it? Second Chronicles 7:14 is still true: "If My people who are called by My name will humble themselves, and pray and seek My face, and turn from their wicked ways, then I will hear from heaven, and will forgive their sin and heal their land."

God's people must say, "Oh, God, it is me. God, I have sinned." They must pray and seek His face and cry out as David did and immediately turn from their wicked ways.

Dear people of God, please listen. God wants to see His people acknowledging that their sin is as serious as He says it is. He wants to hear that we are determined that sin will not reign in us. God wants to see us on our knees crying out to Him:

Oh, God, forgive me. God, I've not been the father I should have been to my children, and I know what I'm supposed to be, but I've quenched Your Holy Spirit when You told me to guide my children. Oh, God, You have told me that I should pray and heaven would hear me, but I've not prayed. Oh, God, You have told me to go out and share with those who do not know You, but I have not shared. Oh, God, You have told me to seek Your ways, and I've not sought them. Oh, God, I have sinned against You. But, oh, God, if You would have mercy on me and withhold from me what I rightly deserve because of this, then, oh, God, I will serve You with all of my heart.

The Scripture says that if we will respond, then God will hear from heaven and will forgive our sin. And then, do you know what will happen next? Then the great healing of America will begin to take place. When God's people return, then the presence filling the people of God will be so powerful in the hand of God that multitudes will come under the conviction of their sin—because they see God's people serious about their sin. Then they will say, "If judgment is beginning at the house of God, what chance do we have?"

It is amazing that in the great revival in Wales—when a hundred thousand came to know the Lord in six months, and it turned the world upside down—a sermon preached to lost people was rarely heard. The sermons preached were to God's people. But when the world saw God's people realizing how serious sin was in their lives, it brought them under severe conviction of their own sin, and atheists and agnostics watching God's people confess their sin and getting their lives right cried out, "Oh, me too! If that person cries out to God and realizes how serious it is, how much more do I need to cry out?" There is written testimony of agnostics coming to know Christ in the middle of a meeting where God's people realized the seriousness of their sin, and the agnostics cried out to God, "Oh, God, have mercy on me! Blot out my transgressions. Wash me thoroughly. Cleanse me. Deal with me. Create in me a clean heart, O God, and renew a steadfast spirit within me."

The Scripture says that if we will respond, then God will hear from heaven and will forgive our sin. And then, do you know what will happen next? Then the great healing of America will begin to take place.

If we would cry unto God, there is no question that God would suddenly fill our lives with His mighty presence, and there would be an immediate response of God's working through us to touch others. But the greatest single concern I have is what we have done to His name. I repent not for what it has done through my life but what it has done to Him. "Oh, God, how could I have done this to Your Son? How could I have done this to Your Holy Spirit? How could I have done this to You who, through the blood of Your Son, made a covenant with me that I would be set apart to be Yours. How could I have done this to You? Oh, God, have mercy."

Three

A HIGHWAY OF HOLINESS

A highway shall be there, and a road,
And it shall be called the Highway of Holiness.
The unclean shall not pass over it,
But it shall be for others.
Whoever walks the road, although a fool,
Shall not go astray.
No lion shall be there,
Nor shall any ravenous beast go up on it;
It shall not be found there.
But the redeemed shall walk there,
And the ransomed of the LORD shall return,
And come to Zion with singing,
With everlasting joy on their heads.
They shall obtain joy and gladness,
And sorrow and sighing shall flee away.

ISAIAH 35:8–10

This was an awesome moment when God spoke to Isaiah. Isaiah spoke about a time when God would establish a highway and it would be called *the highway of holiness*. God has not changed His agenda. Holiness is a highway for God. God has helped me to understand something of what that means. I have watched the Lord deal with my own life, but I have also watched the Lord create a highway over which He is passing.

REVIVAL IN BROWNWOOD

In 1996 I was in Brownwood, Texas, with Pastor John Avant. We spent four awesome days in the presence of God. Holiness was so evident there. The people who were present absolutely could not stand in the holiness of God but instantly confessed enormous sin—in settings that would not be normal for them. The next morning when John arrived at his office, one of his laymen stood at his door weeping and said, "Pastor, I've just got to repent." There were great dimensions of his life that had been radically exposed. Sunday night possibly twenty different kinds of churches spontaneously closed their services and came to the place where God was moving. If you were to ask them, they would not have been able to tell you why they came. The presence of God had drawn them. And as the invitation was extended spontaneously, such weeping and utter brokenness happened before the Lord. Although people came from different denominations, it seemed as if they were one people with a terrible sense of what it means to stand in the presence of a holy God—in God's presence all sin is exposed.

Could I dare say to you that wherever else you are, you are not in the presence of God if sin is not being exposed? You may simply be practicing religion if sin is not exposed. You will know when you stand in the presence of a holy God. When the Word of God is shared, it is different from when the Pharisees shared the Scriptures. When the Spirit of God takes the Word as a sword, the Spirit of God divides down to the soul, spirit, bone, and marrow. God's Word is an absolute "discerner of the thoughts and intents of the heart" (Heb. 4:12), and it openly exposes the heart to a holy God. You will know when the Spirit of God is wielding the Word of God.

God has held my life accountable to that. I must make sure that I am accountable to God. I might need to survey my own heart by saying, *Henry, don't keep saying that the Spirit of*

God is wielding the Word of God if sin can stay rampant in the life of everybody who hears God's Word from you. Don't keep fooling yourself. Your life is not a highway over which God is going. Your life is not a highway of holiness except when the Word of God in the hand of the servant of God acts like a sword. If there is no exposure of sin when we preach, there is something wrong with our lives in their holiness. The Scripture says that when God builds a highway, it is a highway of holiness!

It had been an awesome few days as we spent time before the Lord, and then opened the Word of God, and then watched it begin to move in ways I had not seen before. I had had a deep burden for college students. We were on the campus of Howard Payne University for three days and nights. Tuesday night, when we finished presenting the Word of God, John and I watched to see not what we could do for God, but what God was doing in the midst of His people. John had said, "Lord, if there's anybody that You have touched deeply that may need to share, would You bring him or her to me? I will not seek it out nor will I manipulate it."

Two young men came on their own initiative. They were broken. They had been in a time of prayer. For several weeks spontaneous prayer groups had broken out all over the campus. You could walk on that campus almost anywhere and see somebody praying. All across the dormitories, without any announcement, there were prayer groups. Some of them went through the night, into the early morning. I must have had twenty students talk to me about a different prayer group that was meeting and ask if I wanted to join them. Some were in the tower, one was in a basement, one was in a dorm room, and some were in the chapel. There was a spontaneous sense that God in His holy presence had chosen to be there.

Tuesday night when we had finished sharing, we asked these two young men if they would share. Both were outstanding leaders on the campus. One began in grave brokenness. He shared that he had been in bondage to pornography and lust. You could almost hear a gasp because these young men had been looked up to as leaders. They began to pour out their hearts explaining how they had been impure in their lives, and how it had shut down their prayer lives, and how they had a form of godliness—but all the power was gone. They had no power when they prayed and no power when they opened the Word of God.

They began to pour out their hearts for God to have mercy on them, cleanse them, and make them pure and holy. With tears and brokenness, they began to talk about a deep desire for holiness in their lives. I turned and simply said, "Then if God has laid that on your heart and you have openly acknowledged that you have deeply sinned against God, would you just go over there and pray? Are there others of you young men who have allowed pornography and lust and sin to grip your life and your heart? Would you come and pray?" It was like a steady stream, and then an avalanche. Students from all over that great auditorium began to come, and they filled the whole platform area—weeping, sobbing, and crying out to God.

Later, one after another, they began to unfold the incredible sin that had gripped their hearts. They would begin by saying, "I have been a Christian since I was young. I've grown up in the church," or, "I'm a pastor's child," or, "I'm a missionary's child," and then they would pour out their hearts. Many of the young men turned to the young women and said, "Though I've not actually had sex with anybody, I just want you to know that I have defiled you with my mind and my actions." A number of them said, "You girls, I ask you to forgive me. I just want you to know that I am so sorry for what I have been and what I have done." And they would just collapse on the platform in brokenness. The sin was incredible.

Then an attractive, young female student came and said, "You're saying it's just the men. Well, we women also have lust in our hearts." Then to my amazement, as she was describing with brokenness the sin in her heart, she said, "I ask you fellows to forgive me for the way I've dressed. I have not dressed like a Christian should dress. I ask you men to forgive me. Please forgive me. My heart and my mind and my life have been so full of sin."

I said to her, "I want you to go over to the piano and pray. Are there any other of you young women who are tired of your sin and you want to come and ask God to sweep across your mind and your heart and your life? Would you come?"

The pastor was behind the screen. He said, "I thought I heard a thundering crowd."

Those girls just ran to the platform, and they began to sob even before they got there. They went to one another and they wept.

Adults were there also. I said to the adults, "Are there some of you who need to come and pray?" One of the men who came was a pastor. His son was a student at the university.

He looked over and said, "Son, I have been a model before you, but before God and each of you, you need to know that I, too, have had lust and pornography in my mind and in my heart as a pastor." He said, "Son, forgive your dad. I've not been able to be the spiritual leader that God intended me to be." There was deep brokenness as God dealt with him.

I said, "Sir, you need to come down here. There may be other adults that would come."

I thought to myself as I was listening and weeping along with them: *The highway of holiness is something God creates, but when God creates a highway of holiness He exposes sin like a refiner's fire.*

Three-and-a-half hours later I said, "There may be some who need to leave."

The pastor later told me, "Henry, there were people on their faces before God all night long. They never went to bed."

Tuesday we had a noon luncheon, and it was full. There were maybe twenty or twenty-five different denominational groups, business people, and key people present. We were just about to close our time together when the dear pastor wisely said, "Now before we bring our benediction, is there anyone who would like to speak to God in confession of your sin?"

Some pastors in that group began to cry out, "Oh, God, my mind is so full of filth! My heart is so full of sin and lust!" We were standing, waiting to finish, and people all over began to acknowledge that they had sinned grievously against God.

I waited a long time and then talked to people afterward. A little elderly lady with two canes feebly made her way up to me. When she looked at me, tears streamed down her face. She said, "I'm eighty-eight years old, and I desire purity before God more than anything in all the world. Do you think God could make me clean and use me at eighty-eight?"

I said, "Young lady, God's about to give you the best days of your life. God is creating a highway of holiness for you."

"Oh," she said, "I desire holiness more than anything in the world!"

What I see happening is that God is creating a *highway of holiness*. And I say with all the reverence of my soul—*the unclean will not walk on it!* They will not! It is for others. It is for those who understand the awesome holiness of God! I believe we have a generation that has no experience of or reference point to revival. We also have a generation that has almost no reference point to a genuine experience of the holiness of God. You cannot talk about the holiness of God without, at the same time, the refiner's fire touching every corner of your life, leaving it absolutely exposed to Him. When you read the Word of God, it's like a hammer. The Word of God is like a blaze. You cannot turn anywhere without everything in your heart and life being exposed to God. The holy God does not play games. If you have a heart that is hard, you can walk into His presence with a mind filled with

What I see happening is that God is creating a *highway of holiness.* And I say with all the reverence of my soul—*the unclean will not walk on it!* They will not!

videos and TV programs, and it will never bother you—no grief anymore, no sorrow, no turning it off.

FAITHFUL TO GOD'S WORD

I was in Nairobi with our missionaries not long after the Rwandan crisis, and as best I knew how, I sought to be faithful to the Word of God. Everyone who hears you speak knows whether you have come from the presence of God. God is not allowing His people to fail to recognize whether it is only a sermon or a word from God. God is very serious. There is a sense that God is heightening the hunger and thirst in the hearts of His people. Before you speak on God's behalf, you need to have that Word washed over your own heart and life.

All of this was going through my heart and mind as I was about to speak to our Rwandan missionaries. They had seen such horrible things. They had cried unto God. Many pastors, their dear wives, and their children had been killed. I knew that the missionaries came from South Africa to Ethiopia. Some had been in prison, some had friends who had been killed, and some of them had been wounded in the battles. One of the missionary wives who came had had a number of soldiers break into her house. The soldiers had beaten up her husband and then raped her repeatedly while her little children were in the back of the house. And now she was being tested for AIDS.

I do not know about you, but when I am speaking to a group of frontline warriors, I tremble! I said, "Oh, God, when I open this Book, I tremble. These dear people need to see the blazing holiness of God, because they are filled with what sin can do. They are immersed in what sin can do, but, oh, God, somehow they need to stand in Your presence." So I took the Bible and began to share. It was one of those rare and wonderful moments. I believe there will be no revival without holiness in the leadership. None. Cry unto God all you want. He will not hear you. Pull together all the phrases that revivalists of other generations have all quoted, and it will not make an ounce of difference to the heart of God. God is looking for holiness!

While I was sharing with our dear missionaries, I said, "Who am I to be here?" That was one of those times I wished there was another one who could be speaking and I could listen and cry with them. But I was the one who was speaking.

I was faithfully opening the Word of God and taking the verses and saying, "See *this* God, see this? That's your God. That's Him. He's with you." Suddenly one of the men jumped up and began to weep right in the middle of my sharing, and he said, "Oh, God, I need holiness in my life." I hadn't even talked about holiness. I hadn't even mentioned it. But I did bring him through the Word of God into the presence of a holy God.

Suddenly others began to get up, and they said, "Oh, I ask for holiness in my life too."

Then one of our missionaries began to say, "I'm going to go home and trash every video that we have in our home. Since we don't get TV, we bought videos, and we were not at all careful with what we bought. There's so much we've let our children see. We said, 'It's just got a little blasphemy in it, but it's a good story line.'"

That is like saying *No, Lord!* There is no such thing as a little blasphemy that has a good story line. Those cancel each other out. You just removed the good story when you filled it with blasphemy. I have heard a lot of pastors say, "Well, it has good moral truths in it, a little blasphemy here, a little sin there." If you put that in your heart I can guarantee you,

God will not hear you when you pray. He absolutely will not. An impure mind and heart does not even know how to pray.

I have found that I cannot pray when there is sin in my life. Oh, I can make some words but I just want to hang my head in shame and say, *Oh, God, You knew that everything I said was to cover the sin that I have not been willing to deal with in my life. I just let it run across my life, and I've excused it.* But the Lord does not let you do it. All through those missionary times, there was a spontaneous sense of the holiness of God, and a return to a godly life and a pure life.

There is no such thing as a little blasphemy that has a good story line. Those cancel each other out.

When their hearts were right, many of them instantly realized that they were mistreating their wives—those holy gifts from God, chosen for them from before the world.

I told my wife, "Marilynn, when I knelt at the altar to marry you, I was scared half to death."

"Oh," she said, "I wasn't. I was having a good time."

I said, "That bothered me. You were having such a wonderful time."

She said, "Well, why did you feel so scared?"

"Oh," I said. "Let me tell you why. Do you know when God had a purpose for your life? Before the world was made! For twenty-one years the holy God was shaping your life. He put Scriptures into your heart as a little girl. He caused you to feel the call of missions when you were a young girl involved in a missions education program. He took you to college, and He shaped your life for Himself, and then He took that tender, precious, clean life and He gave it to me. When I was at the altar, I said, *Oh, God, help me to guide her as Your servant.*" And then I said, "Marilynn, tell me every commitment you have ever made to God. I'll spend the rest of my life helping you fulfill those commitments." I have held her life as a sacred trust.

When those missionaries came into the presence of a holy God and faced Him, God began to wash them with the Scriptures specifically and deeply to turn their minds, hearts, wills, and souls against what had been so offensive to Him. The men looked around and the moment their eyes saw their dear wives, they wept their hearts out. They knew they had not treated them well. Suddenly they were looking at their wives as a sacred trust they had mishandled, and they began to weep.

With increasing intensity I have seen that of absolute necessity, the highway over which revival comes, is the *highway of holiness*. Since God is holy, our lives must be holy.

REVIVAL PRAYING

I have been in many meetings that had a focus on a heart cry for revival. My own heart has had a cry for revival since I was a young teenager, and God put me in a nation where the brokenness for revival was laid on my heart at a very young age.

Psalm 24 needs to be applied when praying for revival:

> Who may ascend into the hill of the LORD?
> Or who may stand in His holy place?
> He who has clean hands and a pure heart,
> Who has not lifted up his soul to an idol,
> Nor sworn deceitfully.
> He shall receive blessing from the LORD,

And righteousness from the God of his salvation.
This is Jacob, the generation of those who seek Him,
Who seek Your face. Selah

Lift up your heads, O you gates!
And be lifted up, you everlasting doors!
And the King of glory shall come in.
Who is this King of glory?
The LORD strong and mighty,
The LORD mighty in battle.

Lift up your heads, O you gates!
Lift up, you everlasting doors!
And the King of glory shall come in.
Who is this King of glory?
The LORD of hosts,
He is the King of glory. Selah

PSALM 24:3–10

Who can ascend the hill of the Lord? And who can stand in His holy place? "He who has clean hands and a pure heart, who has not lifted up his soul to an idol, nor sworn deceitfully.

He shall receive blessing from the LORD, and righteousness from the God of his salvation" (vv. 4–5).

I am deeply convinced that praying for revival is an offense to God if we do not have a clean heart. It is almost blasphemy to dare to come into the presence of a holy God and ask Him to bless us when our hearts are not clean before Him. Praying for revival has a prerequisite. Who can ascend the hill of the Lord? Who can stand in His holy place? Who can stand in His presence? Who can stand in the throne room—*the most holy place*—as Hebrews 10 describes it?

One of the great deterrents to revival and awakening is that we do not hold ourselves accountable. We read the Word of God but do not hold ourselves accountable to see it implemented in our lives. This Scripture says that if we meet the conditions of holiness in our lives, He will bless us.

Are you looking to see if there is an obvious touch of God through your life and ministry? Do you minister week after week—yet not one of God's people comes under conviction? Do you talk to the leaders in your church knowing they are full of sin and yet they have absolutely no sense of the holiness of God? How can a holy man stand in their presence and they not feel the presence of God? The Scripture says that when our lives are what God wants them to be, there will be an obvious open blessing of God.

There have been times I have wept and wept before the Lord and said, *Lord, I'm a sinner at best, and You're going to have to work through my life until I'm at least somewhere near where You want me to be. I'll know that I'm in the right relationship with You if You begin to work through my life to implement obviously and openly in the hearts of people what You said You would do.*

But we do not seem to hold ourselves accountable. We do not seem to say, *Well, I'm going now to look to see if anything is happening, and if nothing is happening, I will be deeply grieved in my heart. I will not be able to stand it if God has not done a work in me so that He can do a work in the hearts of His people.*

I talk with so many pastors who describe their churches as being rebellious and disoriented to God. A question I ask them is, "How long have you been there?"

Many reply, "I've been there five—or even seven, ten, or fifteen—years."

I reply, "Then the people in the church are the product of your walk with God. You ought not to have been with a people for five years or more and the holiness of God not absolutely come over the people. The holiness of God should be so real in your own heart that when you get up to speak, there is a sense of holy awe that you have been in the presence of God."

We sometimes say we have been in the presence of God, but everything God says will happen when we are in His presence is absent—and we do not hold ourselves accountable. I feel that it is time for us to say, *It's me, oh, Lord.* If there is nothing happening that God says will happen when His servant is where God wants him to be, then we ought to be grieved of heart. We ought to have a brokenness of spirit that would say, *Oh, God, I will not rest. I cannot rest at night unless I know that this servant is what You want him to be. I'll know that I am when I start to walk among Your people and there is an obvious encounter with You that cannot be explained except with a sense that the awesome presence of God is in my life.*

Do you hold yourself accountable as the servant of God? Do you look at the Scriptures and then say, *If God says this, then this is what will come when a person walks with God?* I tell the people that I walk with Him. Tell your people that whatever they see in the Scriptures that God says will happen through a person that walks with Him, will happen! Please do not excuse the fact that none of this is happening in your life and then tell the people, *But I'm a God-called man.* I will not stand telling someone that I have a word from God if I do not. If I have not let that word come through my life, I will not speak.

There is incredible hunger in the hearts of God's people. The moment a person who walks with God opens the Word of God, you do not have to worry whether they are going to reject repentance. In the last few years when I have spoken on repentance, I have seen the altars filled with God's people dealing with their sin. I have watched pastors, laypeople, youth, and college students come. I have watched them come in absolute brokenness before the Lord. It may be hard to believe, but I have not had one word of criticism from the people of God to whom I spoke concerning repentance. They say, *We've been waiting for somebody to tell us what to do. Our hearts are so full of sin, and we didn't know how to break the bondage of that.*

If I could have gathered up all the brokenness and sin those college students at Howard Payne confessed, it would have been a mountain. I shared with the faculty by saying, "Some of you professors, if these same children—these same young people—can be in your classes week after week and still carry that utter brokenness of sin, there's something wrong with your teaching. These students are right now weeping their hearts out saying, 'I would have given anything if someone had helped me get rid of this awful sin a year ago. I've got such brokenness in my life, and it is accumulating, and nobody seemed to even confront it.'" I then turned to the pastors and said, "Do you recognize any of these students?

> There is incredible hunger in the hearts of God's people.

Do you know they have been sitting in your churches week after week after week?" There's something wrong with our preaching and our worship if the young people of our day can be filled so full of sin and we not have any impact on that sin whatsoever.

As pastors we should each grieve before the Lord and say, *Oh, Lord, if Your people can walk in sin and listen to me preach week after week without a change, then there's something wrong with this preacher. Not with them, with me. What is it that's missing in my life? What is it in my life that God is not honoring? What is it that God says He will not do until some things are in place in my own life?*

HOLINESS AND THE JUDGMENT OF GOD

Psalm 24 fits well in the midst of a passage in James. Psalm 24:3 says, "Who [can] stand in His holy place?" Then in James 5 this Truth is given: *It is the very active prayer of a righteous person that is very powerful in his working.* Is not that true? Do you know what I believe to be one of our greatest dangers? We have all the Truth in our heads, but it has never touched our hearts. Do you know how you can tell if the Truth has touched your heart? According to Jesus it is spiritually impossible to have your heart in one condition and the fruit of your life in another condition. If we can say that we believe the Truth from the Word of God and say that those Truths are in our hearts and yet see no evidence of the implementing of those Truths in our lives, then the Scripture has just been in our heads and it has never struck our hearts.

You will know when the Truth has gone from your head to your heart if there is such a change in your life that the implementing of the Truth is obvious to you and to everyone else. You will know if the Truth has reached your heart if it is bearing fruit in your life. When it bears fruit in your life then it will bear fruit in a world around you.

We have conditioned ourselves to fill our heads with Truth. We think that because we believe the Bible correctly that all the Truth is implemented in our lives.

If you were to talk to many pastors and say, "Do you believe in prayer?" many would say, "Absolutely."

Then you could ask, "Do you pray?"

They might answer, "Well, that's been the weak point of my life."

I would have to say, "Your problem is you. You do not believe in prayer. You do not believe in the God who issues a summons to come before Him. You have the Truth in your head, but it has never reached your heart."

Have you ever been summoned by God into His holy presence? Has He issued a summons to you? Did you come into His presence when He summoned you? Did you stay there until God had transformed you with His Word? Has that Word so changed you in your heart that people wondered what in the world had happened to you? That is when the Truth that comes from the mouth of God has gone from your

84

head to your heart. Because when it is assimilated in your heart, then it impacts the way you live. Jesus taught that what you see coming out of a person is the indication of his heart. We keep walking with the Truth saying, *I believe in revival. I believe in awakening.* But did you hear that Scripture that was read from Joel? "'Now, therefore,' says the LORD, 'Turn to Me with all your heart, with fasting, with weeping, and with mourning.' So rend your heart, and not your garments; return to the LORD your God, for He is gracious and merciful, slow to anger, and of great kindness; and He relents from doing harm" (Joel 2:12–13). I do not know what you do about that Scripture, but let me tell you what I do. Did you hear this command of God? What did He tell the Levites to do? *Wail. Mourn. Grieve.* That is a command. We have it in our heads, but it has never touched our hearts. You will know when it hits your heart. You will cry like Jeremiah did: "Oh, that my head were waters, and my eyes a fountain of tears, that I might weep day and night for the slain of the daughter of my people!" (Jer. 9:1).

We can read and identify the book of Joel with America and never respond to the command of God. It is the spiritual leaders who must grieve. Now, when you read Joel 2:12–13, what do you do with it? It is a command and it is a prerequisite for God's withholding His hand of judgment. Do you believe that if we will not follow that command, the judgment of God will come? I have said to myself, *Oh, Lord, what have I done when I've stood in Your holy presence? You are a holy God. The way of revival is the way of holiness. That means anytime You speak, I bring my life into Your presence and let You change it. You match my heart with Your heart.*

We have been using the right terminology about revival but have not let it penetrate our hearts. When was the last time the pain was so heavy in your heart that you could not bear it? When was the pain so grievous to you that you could not find words to speak? I do not know about you, I just know what God is doing in my life. God is saying, *Henry, it's time for accountability. Don't you ever come to My Word and see what I say and not make certain it goes from your head to your heart to your life to the rest of the world around you.* We must be willing to let God come as a refiner's fire—a launderer's soap—until He has refined us like silver and gold.

In James 5:17–18 the Scripture shares that Elijah was a man who had a nature just like yours and mine. But there was a difference—he prayed. Well, that is half the difference. What is the most important difference? When he prayed, God did something. Have you been praying for revival? Most of you would say, *Amen*. What evidence do you see that God has heard you? Does it bother you? Does America need revival? Has God put it on your heart to pray for revival? Has it ever gripped you, or have we gone away from the command of God that says, "The prayer of a righteous man is powerful and effective" (James 5:16 NIV)? Elijah prayed and it did not rain. Then Elijah prayed and it did rain and the whole of Israel was brought back to God. If you understand that Scripture, does it bother you when you pray but nothing happens? I have gone before the Lord and said, *Lord, I've got to see, not for my sake, not for the people's sake, but for Your name's sake. Lord, it's not a matter of my just praying. It's a matter of my praying and when I have prayed then something happens.*

I went back to 1 Kings 18. This chapter should be a pattern for our praying as well.

And it came to pass, at the time of the offering of the evening sacrifice, that Elijah the prophet came near and said, "LORD God of Abraham, Isaac, and Israel, let it be known this day [number 1] that You are God in Israel [number 2] and I am Your servant [number 3], and that I have done all these things at Your word. Hear me, O LORD, hear me, that this people may know that You are the LORD God, and that You have turned their hearts back to You again.

1 KINGS 18:36–37

Do you hold yourself accountable when God lays that Scripture on your heart? Do you ask, *Oh, God, at which point in this process am I grossly deficient in my walk with You? Is it that I have never heard You say that there will be no rain? Is it that I am not close enough to You to hear or even know what You are asking? Is it that I have not had a word from You so that You will not do anything when I cry? Where in this picture have I not even come close to responding?*

My heart says, *Oh, God, is there not a point in our lives where, if that passage in James is true, then we could follow that pattern and say, "Lord, would You make certain that I understand what it means to be a righteous man, to have holiness as the pattern of my life so that I can stand in Your holy hill? You have dealt with me about sin in my life and the need for holiness to be a part of my life so that when I stand in Your holy place, I know what You say. When I stand in Your holy place, my ears are open, my*

88

eyes are open, and my heart is tender because there is no sin there. You have dealt with my sin radically, and my ears hear Your voice, and my eyes understand what You are doing, and my heart responds. I can go from that moment and say that there is a word from the Lord and You will respond—that the people will know that You are God—and there is at least one servant who is serving You and listening to You and bringing Your word."

You have dealt with my sin radically, and my ears hear Your voice, and my eyes understand what You are doing, and my heart responds.

What was God's response? Did God respond? That is the point at which I want us to be accountable to God. All through the Scriptures God says the *highway* over which He goes, the *highway* over which God's people travel is the *way of holiness*. That is especially true when God brings to our hearts what He wants us to do in prayer. When we pray as God initiates us to and our lives are clean to receive His Word, then He will respond. But if He does not respond, it is at that point that we should hold ourselves accountable. Now, could I put it this way? Did the response of God to Elijah, causing the hearts of His people to return, wait until all the people got their lives right? No, one person got his life right. Then the Scripture says in 1 Kings 18:37: "that this people may know that You are the LORD God, and that You have turned their hearts back to You again."

All over the nation people are finding their hearts returning to God. It is something God does. But my heart cry is to say it is crucial that we hold ourselves accountable to a life of holiness—that if we walk righteously, there will come a response from God. Our lives will be a *highway* over which God shall come.

Remember how John the Baptist preached in Luke 3:4: "Prepare the way of the Lord; Make His paths straight. [Make a highway for our God.]" That highway is the *highway of holiness*. It is a clean and pure heart that sees God. Jesus said, "Blessed are the pure in heart, for they shall see God" (Matt. 5:8). It is that kind of a walk that God uses as the *highway* over which, I believe, He will move mightily in revival. I have been with so many people who have prayed for revival with their lips, but their hearts had not known the cleansing touch of a holy God. I am not saying that to be critical. I know how my own heart was for so long. I know how easy it is for me to say the words and feel that as long as I have a head cry unto God that He will know that I am serious. God says, *You'll know when you have met the conditions of holiness when you see Me start to move in mighty power through your life and through your church and out to the ends of the earth.*

There is one other Scripture I want us to consider; then I want to give a very practical approach to what things are affecting holiness in our lives. Let us read Hebrews 12. There are many places that we could begin. We'll begin with verse 7:

> If you endure chastening, God deals with you as with sons; for what son is there whom a father does not chasten? But if you are without chastening, of which all have become partakers, then you are illegitimate and not sons. Furthermore, we have had human fathers who corrected us, and we paid them respect. Shall we not much more readily be in subjection to the Father of spirits and live? For they indeed for a few days chastened us as seemed best to them, but He for our profit, that we may be partakers of His holiness.

HEBREWS 12:7–10

When I disciplined my children I did so with what I felt was best. But when God chastens, He has a goal in mind. He says that He chastens for our profit that we may be partakers of His holiness. "Now no chastening seems to be joyful for the present, but painful; nevertheless, afterward it yields the peaceable fruit of righteousness to those who have been trained by it. Therefore strengthen the hands which hang down, and the feeble knees" (Heb. 12:11–12). I underlined *the feeble knees*. What does that symbolize? Prayer life. We must strengthen our prayer life deeply and then make straight paths for our feet so that the lame may not be turned aside or dislocated but rather be healed. I held my life up against this Scripture when I was at Howard Payne University that weekend. I said, *Oh, God, would You help me to deal with my walk with You in such a way that those who are stumbling all over the place will not just be turned aside and their knees dislocated, but that they will be healed?*

I do not know how you respond to a Scripture like that, but I said, *Oh, God, I earnestly ask You to deal with me so that the students on this campus will be healed and not hindered in their walk with You.* Then I looked to see if any of the students were being healed, because I did not want to go to the next assignment and say, *Oh, God, do the same thing. You didn't do it for me in the last four times but, Lord, I'm going to ask You to do it again.* I said, *Oh, Lord, I'll know if You have helped me to be the kind of person You want me to be if the chastening You are doing in my mind and heart is that I might be a partaker of Your holiness, so that those whom I relate to can be healed, that someone caught up in pornography can be radically set free, that a person who is caught up in lust can be delivered and stand with joy in the heart.*

So many of those students stood weeping and trying to describe the change that had taken place while they were on the platform. They had come into a cleansing touch of the living Lord. Speak about a lame man dancing—that was what was happening! They didn't know how to describe it. One of the young men just started to say, "I don't know, I'm just so happy. I'm just so free. I feel as though I've been healed!" I said, "My brother, you were. You were healed."

Lord, would You discipline me enough so that I can be a partaker of Your holiness so that when the spiritually lame are present and the Word is shared, that a highway to God is there, and they can go over that highway and come out healed on the inside? If no one is being healed when you preach, the problem is not the

Word of God or those who need to be healed. The problem is within you. But the tragedy is that God has placed so many of us in places of leadership and yet so little healing is being done in the lives of His people. There seems to be no grief over that. There is no broken-ness over that. We say that it is the day in which we live. We put the blame everywhere else. Revival comes through the leaders. When God calls us as He did Elijah and says, "I will fashion you and shape you until you have a message to give and then you, in your walk with Me, can give that

> The tragedy is that God has placed so many of us in places of leadership and yet so little healing is being done in the lives of His people.

message. Then I will hold you accountable to do what I say and they will know that I am God and you are My servant and everything you've done is because I've told you."

Let me ask you, when was the last time God clearly demonstrated His power through your life to the people where you serve? If you have to tell them to follow you, you are in trouble. If you have to claim your authority as the pastor of a church because no one is following you, you are in trouble. Do you know when they will follow you? When God puts it in their hearts to follow you. When God can trust your leadership and when God has a man like Elijah. This verse is enormous if you take it seriously. *Lord, help Your people to know that You turn their hearts back to You.*

I think it is time that we quit blaming the people for not responding. The Scripture says if God has a servant who walks in holiness, He will cause the people's hearts to turn to Him. Do you remember the passage for a father—the last part of Malachi 4? He says He will turn the hearts of the fathers to their children. How would you know clearly if God had completed that act in you? What did He say He would do next? He would turn the hearts of the children to the fathers. Now I just take it very simply: *Lord, I'll know when You have turned my heart to my children sufficiently when I see You turning the hearts of my children back to me. And I will not use that Scripture until I see that happening.*

Some of you have children who are a long way away from the Lord, and you have prayed for them. You must stay there in the presence of God until He makes you what He says is a prerequisite for you to turn your hearts to your children. It is a massive thing He does when He turns the heart of the father to his children. It is not just trying to give them attention and calling them every Saturday night. It does not mean He turns your head toward your children; He turns your heart toward your children. You will know when God has turned your heart sufficiently to your children when you see the hearts of your children being turned back to you by God.

I have not heard many preach on this as one of the prerequisites for spiritual awakening. In Luke 1:17 God puts it this way: "He will also go before Him in the spirit and power of Elijah, 'to turn the hearts of the fathers to the children,' and the disobedient to the wisdom of the just, to make ready a people prepared for the Lord." I am convinced that one of the great prerequisites for revival is what He does with the men toward their families. He makes ready a people prepared for the Lord.

Therefore strengthen the hands which hang down, and the feeble knees, and make straight paths for your feet, so that what is lame may not be dislocated, but rather be healed.

Pursue peace with all people, and holiness, without which no one will see the Lord: looking carefully lest anyone fall short of the grace of God; lest any root of bitterness springing up cause trouble, and by this many become defiled; lest there be any fornicator or profane person like Esau, who for one morsel of food sold his birthright.

HEBREWS 12:12–16 NKJV

Do you think there are some spiritual leaders who for one sexual moment of immaturity have sold their spiritual birthrights? I am very disturbed by the number of people who try to get sexually immoral people, who say they have repented, back into the ministry. I am very hard on that. Anyone who can do that has a character flaw. God can forgive your sin, but it takes Him a while to do something with your character— and we are defiling many. We need to let the Word of God become very clear. Many who have been sexually immoral now want to come back saying, *God forgave me,* yet there is absolutely *no* evidence of repentance whatsoever. I am concerned about what we are doing with these situations.

Can you imagine applying that same thinking to Esau? *Well, he repented. Well, he tried to get his birthright back.* That is exactly right, but it was not given back to him. *He sought it with tears.* That is right, but he did not get it back. Holiness says that God is holy, and we have plenty of evidence in the Scripture of the nature of that holiness. This Scripture says Esau sold his birthright for a morsel of food. You know that afterward, when he wanted to inherit the blessing, he was rejected for he found no place for repentance, though he sought it diligently with tears. That is connected with the holiness of God.

The Scripture says we need to pursue holiness. That is, we need to let the full measure of the nature of God become the pattern for our characters. We need to let Him form in us the full measure of the righteousness of Christ. We need to let Him take every part of our minds and our hearts and keep them holy unto Himself. If there are things we keep putting into our minds so that when we go to pray, we cannot pray, then do not pray for revival, because He will not grant it. When the one who walks consistently in his relationship to God stands in God's presence, the character and holiness of God absolutely overwhelms him.

Does the holiness of God overwhelm you? Do you find yourself trembling when God speaks? The other day I turned in the Word and when I read it, there literally came over my life a total trembling from top to bottom. I found myself spontaneously weeping. I found myself literally trembling. I said, *Oh, God, suddenly You made me aware how holy You are and how sinful I am and how much is at stake when I handle the sacred things. When I take this Book I am made aware of how much of eternity hangs in the balance and when I speak with people how much You have in Your heart. Lord, I am totally unworthy of that. Oh, God, if this is true then don't let me ever speak again in Your name. Your holiness and my sinfulness are so far apart.*

Does the holiness of God overwhelm you? Do you find yourself trembling when God speaks?

I lay there without any strength. I said, *Oh, God, how could I possibly speak?* He said, *I'll do in you what I did in Isaiah.* He had no right to speak either, but I took some coals and put them on his lips—and you'll know if I've done it.

I said, *Then, Lord, hold me accountable for holiness. Lord, don't let me just talk about it. Don't let me just read about it, because You said it was the highway of holiness that would bring the people back to You and they would rejoice and they would sing.*

Many of our church services sound like funerals. I have watched some congregations sing praise songs, and if you looked at them five minutes later you would think you were in a funeral service. Praise songs are no substitute for a clean heart. We are leaving people in a terrible condition and some-how we need to have lives that walk in holiness with Him.

Holiness is the highway over which God brings revival. Without holiness no one shall see the Lord. No one can stand in His holy place without clean hands and a pure heart. It is the pure in heart who see God. May the Spirit of God teach us when we pray, not to say, *Oh, God, help me to see You,* with-out saying at the same time, *Oh, God, give me the conditions of heart that are prerequisite to seeing You. I cannot ask You to make Yourself real to me unless I also ask You to do a work of cleansing in my heart and in my mind and in my will, because only then will I ever see You. To ask You to let me see You in all of Your glory without the prerequisite is absolute foolishness.* He will not do it.

I wonder why we have cried unto the Lord and seen so little. Could it be that God is waiting for His servants to walk over the *highway of holiness* to God? The unclean will not walk on it. The clean—those the Lord has ransomed and redeemed from all of our sin, dressed us in His righteousness, and who are now free in heart and mind before Him—will!

I wonder why we have cried unto the Lord and seen so little.

Ask God if some measure from the Scripture has been used of God to quicken your heart and your conscience. We are talking about revival. We are talking about the survival of our nation. We are talking about the eternal destinies of others. We are talking about the honor of our Lord. We are talking about His name. We are talking about being His servants. We are talking about the people of God in great distress with nothing happening such as ought to happen when we have been present with them.

Let us say, *Oh, Lord, begin this process. Do whatever You need to do in me.* Do not take this lightly but with an understanding from His Word.

> "And the Lord, whom you seek,
>
> Will suddenly come to His temple,
>
> Even the Messenger of the covenant,
>
> In whom you delight.
>
> Behold, He is coming,"
>
> Says the LORD of hosts.
>
> "But who can endure the day of His coming?
>
> And who can stand when He appears?
>
> For He is like a refiner's fire
>
> And like launderers' soap.
>
> He will sit as a refiner and a purifier of silver;
>
> He will purify the sons of Levi,
>
> And purge them as gold and silver,
>
> That they may offer to the LORD
>
> An offering in righteousness."
>
> MALACHI 3:1–3

That is where we are. Revival waits on the holiness of His people. May God grant you a quickened heart that you may seek holiness with all of your heart. If there is anything that the Spirit of God brings to your mind that must be removed, then would you—with all of your heart for His sake—ask God to deal with you?

Father, in the magnitude of Your grace You have permitted a number of us to be present when we saw what Your holiness would do in a group of profane children of Yours who knew they were in sin but had nothing that would bring them to conviction. Suddenly You began to work in Your people and their lives began to be cleansed and made whole. Their presence began, like leaven, to affect their families and their business partners across the campus. You touched some so deeply that they openly acknowledged the grossness of their sin, but they also stood to give witness to Your grace. Lord, the moment they did, Your holiness fell on a whole group of people. Lord, would You shape our lives as leaders until holiness is characteristic of our lives? We'll know that it is in place by what happens in the lives of those we touch. Now we ask You to guide us through these moments of personal response to You and we ask it in Your name.

Oh, Father, these are most sacred, most holy moments. Somehow we sense that heaven stands hushed. All the work of redemption is focused on our response to Your holiness. The highway that You have purposed waits on our holiness. You have given us a pattern to be holy as You are holy. Forgive us when we have explained it away. Father, in Your Word You have told us that leaders must be blameless. Oh, Lord, do not let us explain that away. May we be blameless as we stand before Your people and before the world. Oh, God, may these days create a mighty highway for You, that out of the holiness of the lives of each of us, You may with mighty power evidence that we have become what You are looking for and that You have heard our cry as we pray in our holiness and that You have granted the requests. May we see the evidence in the lives of Your people in a watching world as they sense the awesome presence of a holy God in and through our lives and ministry. We pray in Your name, Amen.

ABOUT THE AUTHOR

HENRY T. BLACKABY HAS SPENT HIS LIFE IN ministry. He has served as a music director, Christian education director, and senior pastor in churches in California and Canada; his first church assignment was in 1958. During his local church ministry, Dr. Blackaby became a college president, a missionary, and later an executive in Southern Baptist Convention life.

Dr. Blackaby formerly served on staff at the North American Mission Board in Alpharetta, Georgia, as Special Assistant to the President. Through the office of Revival and Spiritual Awakening of the Southern Baptist Convention, he provided leadership to thousands of pastors and laymen across North

America. He also served concurrently as Special Assistant to the Presidents of the International Mission Board and LifeWay Christian Resources for global revival. Dr. Blackaby is now serving as the president of Henry Blackaby Ministries.

In the early '90s, Henry Blackaby became one of North America's best-selling Christian authors, committing the rest of his life to helping people know and experience God.

The author of more than a dozen books, Dr. Blackaby is a graduate of the University of British Columbia, Vancouver, Canada. He has completed his Th.M. degree from Golden Gate Baptist Theological Seminary. He has also received four honorary doctorate degrees.

Henry Blackaby and his wife, Marilynn, have five married children, all serving in Christian ministry. They are also blessed with fourteen grandchildren.

Acknowledgments

To Thomas Nelson Publishers for asking us to share messages that have been meaningful to us

and

Kerry Skinner, who did a lot of work on the preparation of the manuscript.

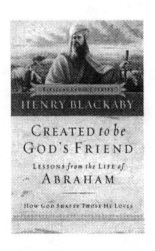

FROM THE EXAMPLE OF THE LIFE OF ABRAHAM, Henry Blackaby will show you how to become God's intimate friend. You will learn how God shapes those He loves into useful, joyful coworkers as they hear and respond to His call in everyday life. *Created to Be God's Friend* is a remarkable study of our relationship with a personal God who is constantly working in each of our lives.

ISBN: 0-7852-6389-6

WORKBOOK ISBN: 0-7852-6391-8

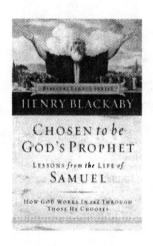

SAMUEL'S LIFE WAS FULL OF INCREDIBLE—AND defining—moments as God shaped him and guided him. As readers observe how God moved in Samuel's life, they will recognize those moments in their own lives; moments that are so different from the run-of-the-mill ones. God uses these "divine moments," which often come during times of crisis, to bring His purposes to pass.

By taking a glimpse into what God did in Samuel's life, Dr. Blackaby enables readers to define those critical times in our lives when God selects us as His chosen servants.

ISBN: 0-7852-6555-4
WORKBOOK ISBN: 0-7852-6557-0

CPSIA information can be obtained at www.ICGtesting.com
Printed in the USA
238736LV00001B/5/A

9 780849 920851